For Maddie B.H.

For Alice,
with all my love,
Mami J.S.

Text copyright © 2006 Bob Hartman
Illustrations copyright © 2006 Janet Samuel
This edition copyright © 2006 Lion Hudson

A Lion Children's Book
an imprint of
Lion Hudson plc
Mayfield House, 256 Banbury Road,
Oxford OX2 7DH, England

www.lionhudson.com

ISBN-13: 978 0 7459 4995 6
ISBN-10: 0 7459 4995 9

First edition 2006
1 3 5 7 9 10 8 6 4 2 0

A catalogue record for this book is available
from the British Library

Typeset in 24/28 BlackheadUnplugged
Printed and bound in China

Noah's Big Boat

Bob Hartman
Illustrated by Janet Samuel

LION
CHILDREN'S

God told Noah it was going to rain
  Rain and rain and rain and pour
So Noah built a boat with a big boat door
  Rain and rain and rain and pour.

God told Noah it was going to rain
   Rain and rain and rain and pour
So Noah took the beasts through
   the big boat door
   Rain and rain and rain and pour.

God told Noah it was going to rain
Rain and rain and rain and pour
So Noah took his family through
the big boat door
Rain and rain and rain and pour.

And then it happened. It started to rain!
Rain and rain and rain and pour
So God himself shut the big boat door
Rain and rain and rain and pour.

It rained forty days and forty nights
   Rain and rain and rain and pour
But not one drop got through the big boat door
   Rain and rain and rain and pour.

The monkeys chattered and the lions roared
Rain and rain and rain and pour
And everyone was safe behind the big boat door
Rain and rain and rain and pour.

The bunnies bounced and the eagles soared
Rain and rain and rain and pour
And everyone was safe behind the big boat door
Rain and rain and rain and pour.

The chipmunk, the cheetah, the bison, the boar
Rain and rain and rain and pour
And everyone was safe behind the big boat door
Rain and rain and rain and pour.

Then the rain just stopped.
   It didn't rain any more.
   Rain and rain and rain and pour
But no one dared open up the big boat door
   Rain and rain and rain and pour.

The big boat floated on a sea with no shore
   Rain and rain and rain and pour
And they all just waited at the big boat door
   Rain and rain and rain and pour.

Then the waters went down –
right down to the floor
Rain and rain and rain and pour

And Noah opened up the big boat door!
Rain and rain and rain and pour.

The monkeys chattered and the lions roared
Rain and rain and rain and pour
And they ran out together through
the big boat door
Rain and rain and rain and pour.

The bunnies bounced
   and the eagles soared
   Rain and rain and rain and pour
And they ran out together through
   the big boat door
   Rain and rain and rain and pour.

The chipmunk, the cheetah, the bison, the boar
Rain and rain and rain and pour
They ran out together through the big boat door
Rain and rain and rain and pour.

Then God sent a rainbow – a promise for sure
"Though it rain and rain and rain and pour
You'll never see a flood like that any more."
Rain and rain and rain and pour.

And Noah walked out through the big boat door.

Other books by Bob Hartman

The Lion Storyteller Bedtime Book

The Lion Storyteller Bible

The Lion Storyteller Book of Animal Tales

The Lion Storyteller Christmas Book